THAI

© 1998 Rebo International b.v., The Netherlands
1998 Published by Rebo Productions Ltd.
Designed and created by Consortium, England
Cover design: Minkowsky, Enkhuizen, The Netherlands
Recipes and photographs © Quadrillion Publishing Ltd.
Godalming, Surrey GU7 1XW
Illustrations by Camilla Sopwith
Typeset by MATS, Southend-on-Sea, Essex
Printed in Slovenia
ISBN 1 84053 044 8
J033uk

THAI

VIBRANT & EXOTIC DISHES, FULL OF FRAGRANT FLAVOUR & VARIETY

 **REBO**
PRODUCTIONS

Contents

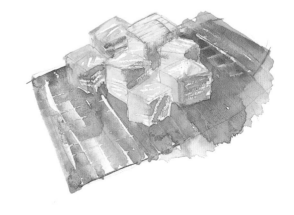

Introduction

Thai food is an exciting medley of flavours and styles which results in a cuisine that, although influenced by the traditional cooking of other countries, remains unique to Thailand.

It is little wonder that Thai food is becoming more and more popular in Western countries. Its flavours are enticing and exhilarating, and not only that, it is quick to prepare and cook. But there is an extra bonus. Thai food is wonderfully healthy, with its predominance of fresh vegetables, emphasis on fish and chicken rather than red meats and use of small quantities of oil.

Authentic tasting Thai food can easily be produced at home. Most of the ingredients are now widely available even from supermarkets, although a good Oriental food store will be stocked with all you will ever need. The cooking techniques involved are simple yet full of variety – stir-frying, steaming, roasting and barbecuing.

Similarities to both Chinese and Indian cuisine are easily recognised, but generally speaking Thai food is hotter and spicier than Chinese and does not involve the long cooking of many Indian dishes.

The selection of recipes in this book exploits the full range of regional specialities and universal popular classics of the authentic cuisine. Whether you are planning an entire Thai meal or simply fancy cooking a Thai-style dish, there is a wealth of interesting recipes on offer. Choose from tempting snacks of crisp pastry-wrapped spiced meats and soups laden with noodles, to sumptuous fish and seafood dishes infused with fresh herbs, hot and aromatic curries and fragrant and flavourful rice and vegetable side dishes. Round off on a refreshing note with exotic fruit-based desserts laced with creamy coconut.

Curry Parcels

These wonton parcels, filled with a spicy chicken and potato mixture, are equally delicious served as a snack or a starter.

Preparation time: 20 minutes • Cooking time: 30 minutes • Makes: 18

Ingredients

225 g (8 oz) chicken breasts	*15 ml (1 tbsp) Red or Green Curry Paste (page 58)*
30 ml (2 tbsp) oil	*10 ml (2 tsp) sugar*
1 small onion, finely chopped	*18 wonton wrappers*
225 g (8 oz) cooked potato, diced	*Oil for deep-frying*

Method

1

Skin the chicken and finely chop. Heat the oil in a wok and stir-fry the onion and chicken for 3 minutes.

2

Stir in the potato, curry paste and sugar, and fry for a few minutes. Remove the chicken mixture to a plate or bowl.

3

Spread the wonton wrappers out on a damp tea-towel, to prevent them drying out too quickly. Spoon a little of the filling into the centre of one of the wrappers.

4

Dampen the edges of the wrapper with water. Pull up the edges of the pastry and pinch together, enclosing the filling. Repeat with the other wrappers until you have used up all the filling.

5

Heat the oil for deep-frying in a clean wok and deep-fry a few parcels at a time for 3-4 minutes, or until crisp and golden.

6

Drain on absorbent kitchen paper and serve immediately.

Serving suggestion

Garnish with slices of cucumber and serve with Sweet-and-Sour Dipping Sauce (page 62).

Variation

Use turkey breast instead of the chicken.

Thai Omelette

In Thailand, omelettes are always served with a hot dipping sauce.

Preparation time: 10 minutes • Cooking time: 10 minutes • Serves: 4

Ingredients

6 eggs	3 spring onions, sliced
30 ml (2 tbsp) fish sauce	30 ml (2 tbsp) oil
5 ml (1 tsp) water	Banana leaves and chilli curls (see 'Cook's tips'), to garnish
1 small red chilli, sliced	

Method

1

Place the eggs in a mixing bowl with the fish sauce and water. Whisk until well combined and slightly frothy. Stir in the chilli and spring onions.

2

Heat the oil in a heavy-based frying pan. When a haze rises from the pan, pour in the egg mixture.

3

Reduce the heat and cook the egg mixture by pulling the egg from the side of the pan as it sets and letting the uncooked mixture run to the edges of the pan.

4

When the egg mixture is almost set, place the pan under a preheated grill to brown the top.

5

Slide onto a serving plate and cut into wedges. Garnish with shapes cut from a banana leaf and chilli curls. Serve with a dipping sauce (see pages 60-64 for recipes).

Serving suggestion

Serve as a quick light lunch dish for 2.

Cook's tips

To make chilli curls, cut the stem off the chilli and shred lengthways. Place in iced water until curled. Banana leaves are available fresh in the refrigerated sections of some Thai grocers, folded up in large plastic bags. Wash well before using.

Thai Spring Rolls (Po Pia Taud)

Spring rolls have become so popular that they are now available in many supermarkets. However, they are simple to make at home, and will taste much better than the supermarket versions.

Preparation time: 20 minutes • Cooking time: 20 minutes • Makes: about 12

Ingredients

30 ml (2 tbsp) oil	5 ml (1 tsp) grated root ginger
1 clove garlic, crushed	15 ml (1 tbsp) chopped fresh coriander
115 g (4 oz) lean pork, chopped	5 ml (1 tsp) fish sauce
2 carrots, cut into matchsticks	55 g (2 oz) cooked noodles
2 sticks celery, cut into matchsticks	About 12 spring roll wrappers
1 red or green chilli, chopped	Oil for deep-frying
4 spring onions, sliced	Fresh coriander leaves, to garnish

Method

1
Heat the oil in a wok or frying pan and fry the garlic, pork, carrots, celery and chilli for a few minutes, until the pork is cooked and the vegetables are beginning to soften.

2
Stir in the spring onions, ginger, coriander, fish sauce and noodles. Cook gently to heat through.

3
Lay out a spring roll wrapper on a clean work surface. Place a little of the filling across one corner of the wrapper. Roll up, folding in the corners to completely enclose the filling. Fill one spring roll at a time, keeping the remaining wrappers covered with a damp tea-towel, to prevent them from drying out.

4
Just before serving, deep-fry the spring rolls in batches for 3-4 minutes, or until crisp and golden. Garnish with fresh coriander and serve immediately.

Serving suggestion
Serve with Sweet Chilli Sauce (page 62).

Variation
Add chopped cooked prawns or bean sprouts to the filling.

Cook's tip
Fish sauce is available from many supermarkets. If unavailable, make your own substitute by pounding together canned anchovy fillets with a little sugar. Add a few spoonfuls of soy sauce and allow to stand for at least 30 minutes. Strain before using.

Beef Saté

This very popular Thai dish combines the complementary flavours of fragrant spices, citrus, chilli and peanuts.

Preparation time: 15 minutes, plus 1 hour marinating time • Cooking time: 10 minutes • Serves: 4

Ingredients

	For the saté sauce
225 g (8 oz) sirloin steak	85 g (3 oz) unsalted roasted peanuts
Grated rind and juice of 1 lime	1 small red chilli
5 ml (1 tsp) chopped fresh chilli	Juice of 1 lime
15 ml (1 tbsp) chopped fresh coriander	1.25 ml (¼ tsp) ground cumin
2.5 ml (½ tsp) ground turmeric	1.25 ml (¼ tsp) ground coriander
2.5 ml (½ tsp) ground cumin	30 ml (2 tbsp) thick coconut milk (see 'Cook's tip', page 32)
30 ml (2 tbsp) fish sauce	30 ml (2 tbsp) oil
Oil for brushing	1 small onion, finely chopped
Chilli flowers and spring onion brushes (see 'Cook's tip'), to garnish	A dash of fish sauce

Method

1

Cut the steak into thin slices and thread onto bamboo skewers. Place in a shallow dish.

2

Mix together the lime rind and juice, chilli, coriander, turmeric, cumin and fish sauce, and pour over the beef.
Turn to coat in the marinade and set aside for at least 1 hour.

3

To prepare the sauce, place the peanuts, chilli, lime juice, spices and coconut milk in a food processor and
process to a paste. Alternatively, grind to a paste with a pestle and mortar.

4

Heat the oil in a saucepan and fry the onion until soft. Stir in the peanut mixture and add some fish sauce to taste.
Add the marinade from the beef and a little water to form a thick sauce. Cook for 5 minutes, stirring constantly.

5

Brush the satés with oil and cook under a preheated grill for 3-5 minutes, or until the beef is cooked through.
Serve with the saté sauce. Garnish with the chilli flowers and spring onion brushes before serving.

Serving suggestion

This is a perfect dish to serve at a party.

Variation

Use crunchy peanut butter in place of the ground peanuts.

Cook's tip

To make chilli flowers, holding a chilli at its stem, slice open lengthways and remove the seeds. Cut through the chilli a few times from just below the stem to the tip. Place in a bowl of iced water for about 1 hour. The ends of the chilli will curl outwards. Spring onion brushes are made in the same way. Trim away the root and the top of the green part, to leave a length about 5-7 cm (2-3 inches). Make cuts from just below the root end to the green end, and place in iced water to make the green ends curl.

Pork Wrapped in Noodles

Relatively mild in flavour, these crisp and golden bundles are enlivened by serving with a chilli-hot dipping sauce.

Preparation time: 20 minutes, plus 30 minutes chilling time • Cooking time: 20 minutes • Serves: 4

Ingredients

225 g (8 oz) minced pork	85 g (3 oz) rice noodles (vermicelli)
5 ml (1 tsp) ground coriander	
15 ml (1 tbsp) fish sauce	Oil for deep-frying
1 small egg, beaten	Whole chillies, to garnish

Method

1
Mix together the pork, coriander and fish sauce until well combined, then add enough egg to bind. Roll the mixture into small balls and chill for 30 minutes.

2
Cover the noodles with warm water and soak for about 10 minutes to soften. Drain the noodles, then wrap several strands around each pork ball.

3
Heat the oil in a wok and deep-fry a few at a time for 3-4 minutes, or until crisp and golden. Drain on absorbent kitchen paper and garnish with whole chillies. Serve immediately.

Serving suggestion
Serve with a hot dipping sauce, such as Nam Prik (page 60) or Sweet Chilli Sauce (page 62).

Variations
Use minced chicken or turkey in place of the pork. Use ground cumin in place of the coriander.

Spicy Prawn Wraps

Use large, uncooked deep-water prawns for this special-occasion dish.

Preparation time: 20 minutes, plus 2 hours marinating time • Cooking time: 12 minutes • Serves: 4

Ingredients

12 raw king prawns	5 ml (1 tsp) grated root ginger
1 clove garlic, crushed	Juice of 1 lime
1 stem lemon grass, finely sliced	12 small spring roll wrappers
1 red chilli, seeded and chopped	Oil for deep-frying

Method

1
Peel the prawns, removing their heads and body shells but leaving the tail fins attached.

2
Remove the dark vein from each prawn. 'Butterfly' the prawns by cutting through the backs of the prawns without cutting right through the bodies. Carefully open the prawns out.

3
Combine the garlic, lemon grass, chilli, ginger and lime juice in a large shallow dish and add the prawns.

4
Turn the prawns so that they are coated in the marinade, then allow to marinate in the refrigerator for 2 hours, turning occasionally.

5
Just before serving, remove the prawns from the marinade and wrap each prawn in a spring roll wrapper, leaving the tail end protruding.

6
Heat the oil to 180°C/350°F in a wok and fry the prawn wraps in batches for 3-4 minutes, or until golden. Drain on absorbent kitchen paper and serve.

Serving suggestion
Serve with a hot dipping sauce, such as Nuoc Cham (page 64).

Cook's tip
Lemon grass imparts a fragrant lemony tang to dishes. To use, cut away the grassy top and hard root, and discard the tough outer leaves. Bruise the stem to release the flavour by pushing down hard on the blade of a knife. Alternatively, as in this recipe, thinly slice the central tender core.

Glass Noodle Soup

This attractive soup contains spicy meatballs and cellophane noodles.

Preparation time: 15 minutes • Cooking time: 15-20 minutes • Serves: 4

Ingredients

30 ml (2 tbsp) oil	30 ml (2 tbsp) fish sauce
2 cloves garlic, thinly sliced	45 ml (3 tbsp) cornflour
55 g (2 oz) dried cellophane noodles	15 ml (1 tbsp) chopped coriander leaves
225 g (8 oz) skinned and boned chicken breast	1 litre (1³/₄ pints) chicken stock
	225 g (8 oz) bok choy, shredded
30 ml (2 tbsp) Green Curry Paste (page 58)	4 spring onions, cut into 2.5-cm (1-inch) pieces

Method

1

Heat the oil in a small frying pan or wok and fry the garlic until golden. Remove with a slotted spoon, drain on absorbent kitchen paper and set aside.

2

Place the noodles in a large bowl and cover with hot water. Allow to soak until softened, then drain.

3

Cut the chicken into cubes, place in a food processor with the curry paste, fish sauce, cornflour and coriander, and process until very finely minced.

4

Remove the mixture from the processor and shape into small balls.

5

Heat the stock in a large saucepan until boiling and add the meatballs. Cook for 10-15 minutes, or until they rise to the surface.

6

Add the softened noodles, bok choy and spring onions, and continue to cook for 5 minutes. Serve sprinkled with the fried garlic slices.

Serving suggestion
Serve on its own as a delicious lunchtime dish.

Variation
Use turkey breast in place of the chicken. Use rice or egg noodles in place of the cellophane noodles.

Cook's tip
Cellophane or glass noodles are made from mung beans and are almost transparent in appearance.

Coconut Prawn Soup

Traditionally, soup is served as part of a full Thai meal.

Preparation time: 20 minutes • Cooking time: 10 minutes • Serves: 4

Ingredients

1 stem lemon grass	*2 red or green chillies, chopped*
225 g (8 oz) raw king prawns	*15 ml (1 tbsp) fish sauce*
1.2 litres (2 pints) fish stock	*225 g (8 oz) skinned firm-fleshed white fish fillets, cut into strips*
4 slices galangal	
4 kaffir lime leaves, shredded	*140 ml (¼ pint) thick coconut milk (see 'Cook's tip', page 32)*

Method

1

Thinly slice a piece of the lemon grass about 5 cm (2 inches) in length.

2

Remove the heads and body shells from the king prawns, leaving just the tail fins in place.

3

Remove the dark vein from each prawn and discard.

4

Heat the stock in a large saucepan until almost boiling and stir in the galangal, lime leaves, lemon grass, chillies and fish sauce. Simmer for 2 minutes.

5

Add the fish strips and prawns, and cook gently for 5 minutes.

6

Stir in the coconut milk and continue cooking until very hot, but do not allow the soup to boil. Serve.

Serving suggestion

Serve garnished with a little seeded and finely chopped fresh red or green chilli.

Variation

Use ginger in place of galangal.

Cook's tip

Galangal is similar in appearance to ginger, but has a milder, more perfumed flavour. Used in the same way as ginger, it is available fresh or dried from Oriental stores.

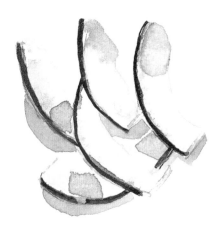

Beef Noodle Soup

You can use any type of noodle in this recipe, or substitute rice for a change.

Preparation time: 15 minutes • Cooking time: 20 minutes • Serves: 4

Ingredients

30 ml (2 tbsp) oil	*2.5-cm (1-inch) piece root ginger, peeled and thinly sliced*
225 g (8 oz) sirloin steak, cut into thin strips	*5 ml (1 tsp) palm sugar*
1 small onion, chopped	*15 ml (1 tbsp) fish sauce*
2 sticks celery, sliced diagonally	*85 g (3 oz) egg noodles*
1.4 litres (2½ pints) chicken or beef stock	*115 g (4 oz) canned straw mushrooms (drained weight)*
15 ml (1 tbsp) chopped coriander stems	*Chilli flowers (see 'Cook's tip', page 14), to garnish*
2 kaffir lime leaves	

Method

1

Heat the oil in a wok or saucepan and fry the steak, onion and celery until the meat
is cooked through and the vegetables are soft.

2

Add the stock, coriander, lime leaves, ginger, sugar and fish sauce. Bring to the boil.

3

Add the noodles and straw mushrooms, and cook for 10 minutes. Serve piping hot, garnished with chilli flowers.

Variation

If you cannot obtain palm sugar – a thick brown sugar available in tubs or cans from
Oriental stores – use an unrefined sugar, such as light or dark muscovado sugar, instead.

Cook's tip

Partially freeze the beef before slicing to make cutting easier. Cut the meat across the grain to keep it tender during cooking.

Grilled Red Snapper

Red snapper is a popular fish in Thailand and can be used for many fish dishes.

Preparation time: 10 minutes, plus 1 hour marinating time • Cooking time: 25-30 minutes • Serves: 2

Ingredients

1 large red snapper, cleaned and scaled	30 ml (2 tbsp) palm sugar
15 ml (1 tbsp) Green Curry Paste (page 58)	3 kaffir lime leaves
150 ml (¼ pint) thick coconut milk (see 'Cook's tip', page 32)	2 stems lemon grass, sliced
	Banana leaf, or baking parchment or foil
45 ml (3 tbsp) fish sauce	Carrot and lemon twigs (see 'Cook's tip'), to garnish

Method

1

Cut 3 or 4 slashes into each side of the fish, and place in a dish. Combine the remaining ingredients, except the banana leaf and garnish, and pour over the fish. Allow to marinate for 1 hour.

2

Place the marinated fish on a piece of blanched banana leaf and pour over some of the marinade. Wrap the fish in the banana leaf until completely enclosed and place in a flameproof dish. Use baking parchment or foil if banana leaves are unavailable.

3

Cook under a preheated medium grill for 25-30 minutes, turning halfway through cooking. Alternatively, bake in an oven preheated to 180°C/350°F/Gas Mark 3 for 30 minutes.

4

Using a pair of scissors, cut a large cross in the banana leaf and serve the fish in the banana leaf, garnished with carrot and lemon twigs.

Serving suggestion

Serve with Thai Steamed Rice (see page 66).

Variation

If lemon grass is unavailable, use a few strips of lemon rind.

Cook's tip

To make carrot and lemon twigs, take a 5-cm (2-in) length of carrot. Cut into thin slices lengthways to form rectangles. Cut rectangles of the same size from the rind of a lemon. Take one slice of carrot and make a cut from each end almost to the opposite end. Repeat with a piece of lemon rind. Twist the outer strips of carrot so that they cross over. Repeat with the lemon rind. In the same way, make twigs with the remaining slices of carrot and pieces of lemon rind. You can also make twigs from slices of cucumber.

Fish Cakes (Taud Man Pla)

Fish cakes are just one of the delicious savouries that you can buy from street vendors in Bangkok, where they make and cook them while you wait.

Preparation time: 10 minutes • Cooking time: 5 minutes • Makes: 8

Ingredients

280 g (10 oz) white fish fillets, skinned	2 spring onions, finely sliced
45 ml (3 tbsp) Red Curry Paste (page 58)	1 egg, beaten
30 ml (2 tbsp) fish sauce	Flour, for dusting
45 ml (3 tbsp) cornflour	Oil for frying
15 ml (1 tbsp) chopped coriander leaves	Carrot and spring onion strips, to garnish

Method

1
Place the fish, curry paste, fish sauce, cornflour and coriander in a food processor and process until very finely minced.

2
Remove the mixture from the processor and beat in the spring onions and enough egg to bind the mixture together.

3
Dust your hands with flour and shape into 8 small rounds. Chill until required.

4
Shallow or deep-fry the fish cakes for a few minutes on each side, until golden. Garnish with strips of carrot and spring onion before serving.

Serving suggestion
Serve with a dipping sauce (see pages 60-64 for recipes) or a chutney of your choice.

Variation
Use cooked crab meat or cooked shelled prawns in place of the white fish fillets.

Steamed Prawns

This dish of simply prepared prawns is quick and easy to prepare and cook yet truly delicious.

Preparation time: 15 minutes • Cooking time: 15 minutes • Serves: 2

Ingredients

450 g (1 lb) raw prawns, in the shell	10 ml (2 tsp) grated root ginger
30 ml (2 tbsp) sesame oil	1 red chilli, sliced
2 cloves garlic, chopped	1 green chilli, sliced
30 ml (2 tbsp) chopped fresh coriander stems and leaves	30 ml (2 tbsp) soy sauce
	Lemon and lime twists, to garnish

Method

1
Wash and shell the prawns.

2
Combine the remaining ingredients, except the garnish, in a small jug or bowl.

3
Place the prawns in a heatproof bowl or plate that will fit into a bamboo steamer. Pour the sauce over and toss well.

4
Place the bowl in the bamboo steamer, cover and steam over a large saucepan or wok of simmering water for 15 minutes, or until the prawns have turned pink and are cooked through.

5
Serve immediately, garnished with lemon and lime twists.

Serving suggestion

Serve with a rice dish such as Thai Fried Rice (page 68) and a hot dipping sauce (see pages 60-64 for recipes).

Cook's tip

Do not overcook the prawns, or they will become tough.

Steamed Fish in Banana Leaves (Haw Mok)

Lining the bamboo steamer with banana leaves, as they do in Thailand, imparts extra flavour to this dish, but you can use baking parchment or foil if banana leaves are unavailable.

Preparation time: 15 minutes • Cooking time: 20 minutes • Serves: 4

Ingredients

450 g (1 lb) white fish fillets, skinned	*2 courgettes, cut into thin sticks*
Banana leaves, or parchment or foil	*150 ml (¼ pint) thick coconut milk*
2 carrots, peeled and cut into matchsticks	*(see 'Cook's tip')*
1 red pepper, cut into strips	*15-30 ml (1-2 tbsp) Red Curry Paste (page 58)*
115 g (4 oz) long beans or French beans,	*2 kaffir lime leaves*
cut into 7.5-cm (3-inch) lengths	*15 ml (1 tbsp) fish sauce*

Method

1
Cut the fish into bite-sized pieces or strips about 1.25-cm (½-inch) wide.

2
Line a heatproof dish which will fit into your bamboo steamer with banana leaves, parchment or foil.

3
Blanch the carrots, pepper and beans for 2 minutes in boiling water, adding the courgettes for the final 30 seconds. Drain and scatter over the banana leaves.

4
Pile the fish on top of the vegetables.

5
Combine the remaining ingredients and pour over the fish. Cover the steamer and steam over a large saucepan or wok of simmering water for 15-20 minutes, or until the fish is cooked through and flakes easily.

Serving suggestion
Serve with Thai Steamed Rice (page 66).

Cook's tip
Coconut milk should not be confused with the juice from the inside of a coconut. Canned coconut milk is available in many supermarkets and from Oriental stores. The coconut milk separates in the can into layers – the top layer, the cream, is very thick and can be scooped off leaving the thin milk underneath. To obtain thick coconut milk, stir the contents of the can together.

Seafood with Egg Noodles

Use any mixture of seafood in this spicy dish, which can be served as a main meal or an impressive side dish.

Preparation time: 15 minutes • Cooking time: 15 minutes • Serves 4

Ingredients

450 g (1 lb) mixed seafood, such as prawns, chunks of fish, squid, clams and mussels	115 g (4 oz) mangetout
	115 g (4 oz) baby corn cobs
3 large green chillies, seeded and chopped	1/2 red pepper, sliced
15 ml (1 tbsp) chopped fresh coriander leaves	15 ml (1 tbsp) fish sauce
2 cloves garlic, crushed	150 ml (1/4 pint) fish stock
175 g (6 oz) fresh or dried egg noodles	15 ml (1 tbsp) lime juice
30 ml (2 tbsp) oil	10 ml (2 tsp) cornflour

Method

1
Cook the seafood separately in boiling water until cooked through, then drain and set aside. If using squid, score the hoods in a diamond pattern before cutting into pieces.

2
Using a pestle and mortar, pound the chillies, coriander and garlic together.

3
Cook the noodles as directed on the packet and set aside.

4
Heat the oil in a wok, add the mangetout, baby corn and pepper, and stir-fry for 4 minutes. Add the chilli mixture and fish sauce, and cook for 2 minutes.

5
Stir in the fish stock and add the cooked seafood and noodles to the pan. Mix the lime juice and cornflour together. Stir into the wok and cook until thickened.

Variation
Use orange or green pepper in place of the red pepper.

Cook's tips
Scoring the squid helps to keep it tender during cooking. Mixed prepared seafood can be bought from large supermarkets, to save preparation time.

Sweet Prawn and Coconut Curry

This is a mild flavoured curry, with the distinctive Thai characteristic of coconut milk.

Preparation time: 10 minutes, plus at least 30 minutes marinating time • Cooking time: 10 minutes • Serves: 4

Ingredients

450 g (1 lb) raw prawns, shelled	4 shallots, sliced
150 ml (¹/₄ pint) thick coconut milk (see 'Cook's tip', page 32)	15 ml (1 tbsp) grated root ginger
	15 ml (1 tbsp) Yellow Curry Paste (page 60)
30 ml (2 tbsp) lime juice	25 ml (5 tsp) palm sugar
30 ml (2 tbsp) oil	Lemon and lime wedges and 15 ml (1 tbsp) toasted desiccated coconut, to garnish
1 clove garlic, crushed	

Method

1
Combine the prawns, coconut milk and lime juice together in a shallow dish. Leave to marinate for at least 30 minutes, stirring occasionally.

2
Heat the oil in a wok and fry the garlic and shallots until softened.

3
Stir in the ginger and curry paste, and stir-fry for 1-2 minutes. Stir in the sugar.

4
Add the prawns and their marinade to the wok, and cook over a reduced heat for 5 minutes, or until the prawns turn pink.

5
Transfer to a serving fish and garnish with lemon and lime wedges. Sprinkle with the coconut and serve immediately.

Serving suggestion
Serve with Thai Steamed Rice (page 66).

Variation
Use king prawns in place of the ordinary prawns.

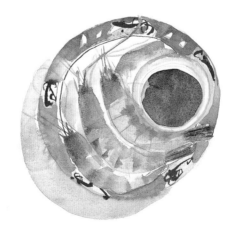

Red Chicken Curry (Gaeng Ped Gai)

Red and green curry pastes are the basis of most Thai curries. This is a simple dish using red curry paste.

Preparation time: 15 minutes • Cooking time: 15 minutes • Serves: 4

Ingredients

450 g (1 lb) chicken breasts, skinned and boned	*300 ml (¹/₂ pint) thick coconut milk (see 'Cook's tip', page 32)*
30 ml (2 tbsp) oil	*115 g (4 oz) canned sliced bamboo shoots (drained weight)*
2 onions, peeled and cut into wedges	
45 ml (3 tbsp) Red Curry Paste (page 58)	*15 ml (1 tbsp) fish sauce*
2 kaffir lime leaves, shredded	*10 ml (2 tsp) sugar*

Method

1

Cut the chicken into bite-sized pieces. Heat the oil in a wok and stir-fry the onions and chicken for 5 minutes, or until the onions are softened and beginning to brown. Remove from the wok and set aside.

2

Add the curry paste and lime leaves to the wok and fry for a few minutes. Stir in half of the coconut milk and boil rapidly for 3 minutes.

3

Return the chicken to the wok and add the bamboo shoots, fish sauce and sugar. Simmer gently for 5 minutes, or until the chicken is cooked. Stir in the remaining coconut milk and cook until heated through.

Serving suggestion

Accompany with Thai Steamed Rice (page 66) and Cucumber Salad (page 84).

Variation

Use turkey breast in place of the chicken. Use shredded lime rind in place of the kaffir lime leaves if they are not available.

Cook's tip

Kaffir lime leaves are shiny and dark green with a distinctive figure-of-eight shape. They are an important flavour in authentic Thai cooking. Used in a similar way to bay leaves, they can be added whole, torn in half or shredded to infuse flavour into the dish, or used as a garnish. They are available fresh, frozen or dried from Oriental food stores.
Dried lime leaves have insufficient flavour, and are best avoided.

Spicy Minced Chicken (Laab Kai)

This version of a traditional Thai dish comes from the north-east of Thailand and contains glutinous rice, which gives it a delicious nutty texture.

Preparation time: 15 minutes • Cooking time: 25-30 minutes • Serves: 4

Ingredients

30 ml (2 tbsp) glutinous rice	15 ml (1 tbsp) oyster sauce
30 ml (2 tbsp) oil	15 ml (1 tbsp) fish sauce
2 cloves garlic, crushed	5 ml (1 tsp) salted black beans
6 small red or green chillies, sliced	30 ml (2 tbsp) soy sauce
350 g (12 oz) chicken, minced	Spring onion slices, to garnish

Method

1

Place the rice in a wok and dry-fry for 5-10 minutes, until the grains are golden on all sides, shaking the wok as it cooks.

2

Pour the toasted rice into a mortar and pound with a pestle until ground almost to a powder.

3

Heat the oil in the wok and fry the garlic and chillies for 2-3 minutes, until softened.

4

Add the chicken and stir-fry, breaking the chicken up as it cooks.

5

Once the chicken is cooked and no longer pink, stir in the oyster sauce, fish sauce, black beans and soy sauce.

6

Add the ground up rice and stir-fry for 2-3 minutes. Serve immediately, scattered with spring onion slices.

Serving suggestion

Serve with Long Beans in Coconut Milk (page 80).

Variation

Use minced turkey in place of the chicken.

Cook's tip

If you don't have a pestle and mortar, place the rice in a plastic bag and crush with a rolling pin.

Pork Curry with Aubergine

This hot and spicy pork curry can be served accompanied with rice for a delicious meal in itself.

Preparation time: 20 minutes • Cooking time: 25-30 minutes • Serves: 6

Ingredients

900 g (2 lb) belly pork slices	85 g (3 oz) long beans, cut into 2.5-cm (1-in) pieces
30 ml (2 tbsp) oil	3 large green chillies, seeded and quartered lengthways
45 ml (3 tbsp) Red Curry paste (page 58)	30 ml (2 tbsp) fish sauce
600 ml (1 pint) water	15 ml (1 tbsp) lime juice
115 g (4 oz) sliced bamboo shoots	5 ml (1 tsp) palm sugar
6 baby white aubergines, quartered	A small bunch sweet basil, torn into pieces

Method

1
Remove the rind from the pork if you like and cut the meat crosswise into 2.5-cm (1-in) chunks.

2
Heat the oil in a wok and fry the curry paste for 2-3 minutes. Add the meat and fry for 5 minutes.

3
Pour in the water and bring to the boil, then reduce the heat and add the bamboo shoots, aubergines, long beans and chillies. Simmer gently for 10 minutes.

4
Stir in the fish sauce, lime juice, sugar and basil, and serve immediately.

Serving suggestion
Serve with Thai Fried Rice (page 68).

Cook's tips
Long beans grow to a length of about 60 cm (2 feet) and are similar in flavour to French or fine beans.
Use the latter as a substitute if you cannot find long beans. Many varieties of small, round aubergines are used in
Thailand. Look for baby white aubergines in Oriental stores, where you might find baby green ones as well.
If unavailable, use ordinary purple aubergine cut into chunks.

Barbecued Chicken

These spicy chicken pieces are delicious served with a hot dipping sauce.

Preparation time: 10 minutes, plus 2 hours marinating time • Cooking time: 10-15 minutes • Serves: 4-6

Ingredients

675 g (1½ lb) chicken thighs	**For the dipping sauce**
30 ml (2 tbsp) Red Curry Paste (page 58)	1 small red chilli, sliced
2 cloves garlic, crushed	1 small green chilli, sliced
150 ml (¼ pint) thick coconut milk (see 'Cook's tip', page 32)	60 ml (4 tbsp) white wine vinegar
30 ml (2 tbsp) chopped coriander leaves and stems	
Banana leaves and chilli halves, to garnish	

Method

1

Place the chicken pieces in a large mixing bowl.

2

Combine the curry paste, garlic, coconut milk and coriander, and pour over the chicken. Toss together until all the chicken pieces are well coated. Leave to marinate for 2 hours.

3

To make the dipping sauce, combine the sliced chillies and vinegar, and set aside until required.

4

Cook the chicken pieces over a preheated barbecue or under a preheated grill for 10-15 minutes, or until tender. Turn frequently and baste with any remaining marinade during cooking.

5

Serve the chicken hot or cold with the dipping sauce. Garnish with shapes cut from a banana leaf and chilli halves.

Serving suggestion

Serve with Stir-Fried Glass Noodles with Chicken (page 76).

Cook's tip

Handle chillies with great care, since their juice is a very strong irritant. It is a good idea to wear disposable or rubber gloves when cutting them. In any case, wash hands very well after preparation. If you prefer a milder flavour, discard the seeds which contain much of the heat. As a general rule, the smaller the chilli, the hotter it will be.

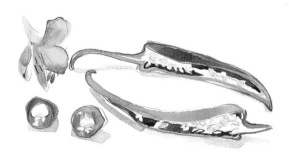

Baked Duck Salad

A delectable and attractive duck dish for a special-occasion Thai meal.

Preparation time: 20 minutes, plus at least 3 hours marinating time • Cooking time: 40 minutes • Serves: 4-6

Ingredients

4 duck breasts	*30 ml (2 tbsp) sesame oil*
5 ml (1 tsp) paprika	*2.5 ml (½ tsp) dried chilli flakes*
312-g (11-oz) can mandarin segments, in natural juice	*115 g (4 oz) flaked coconut*
30 ml (2 tbsp) white wine vinegar	*55 g (2 oz) roasted cashew nuts*
30 ml (2 tbsp) oyster sauce	*Flaked coconut, to garnish*

Method

1

Place the duck breasts on a trivet in a roasting dish and sprinkle with the paprika.

2

Roast in an oven preheated to 200°C/400°F/Gas Mark 6 for 35-40 minutes, or until cooked. Allow to cool and cut into thin slices.

3

Drain the mandarins and reserve the juice. Combine the juice with the vinegar, oyster sauce, oil and chilli flakes.
Pour over the sliced duck and leave to marinate for at least 3 hours.

4

Just before serving, toss the coconut and cashew nuts into the duck and marinade. Transfer to a serving dish and arrange
the mandarin segments in the centre. Serve garnished with a little extra flaked coconut.

Serving suggestion

Serve with Thai Steamed Rice (page 66) to make this dish a meal in itself.

Cook's tip

Duck breasts are available from most large supermarkets.

Green Curry with Beef

A full-flavoured curry made with prime beef steak, baby white aubergines and green curry paste.

Preparation time: 15 minutes • Cooking time: 20 minutes • Serves: 4

Ingredients

30 ml (2 tbsp) oil	4 kaffir lime leaves, torn in half
45 ml (3 tbsp) Green Curry Paste (page 58)	8 baby white aubergines, quartered
350 g (12 oz) sirloin or rump steak, sliced	2 large red chillies, quartered lengthways
425 ml (³/4 pint) thick coconut milk (see 'Cook's tip', page 32)	2.5-cm (1-inch) piece galangal, sliced
30 ml (2 tbsp) fish sauce	5 ml (1 tsp) palm sugar

Method

1

Heat the oil in a wok, add the curry paste and fry for 2 minutes, stirring frequently.

2

Add the beef slices and stir-fry for 2 minutes, or until the meat changes colour.

3

Stir in the coconut milk and fish sauce, and bring to the boil. Boil rapidly for 5 minutes, stirring occasionally.

4

Reduce the heat and stir in the lime leaves, aubergines, chillies, galangal and sugar. Simmer for 5-10 minutes, or until the aubergines are tender.

Serving suggestion

Serve with Thai Fried Rice (page 68) or Sautéed Bean Sprouts (page 82).

Cook's tip

Partially freeze the beef to make cutting easier. Slice the meat across the grain to keep it tender during cooking.

Stir-Fried Chicken with Ginger

This is a classic Thai dish, and appears on many Thai restaurant menus.

Preparation time: 15 minutes • Cooking time: 10 minutes • Serves: 4

Ingredients

30 ml (2 tbsp) oil	2 kaffir lime leaves, shredded
2 cloves garlic, crushed	55 g (2 oz) whole blanched almonds
2 shallots, chopped	115 g (4 oz) long beans, cut into 5-cm (2-inch) lengths
350 g (12 oz) chicken breast, skinned, boned and cut into thin strips	1 red pepper, cut into strips
	85 g (3 oz) water chestnuts, sliced
5-cm (2-inch) piece root ginger, peeled and cut into matchsticks	45 ml (3 tbsp) fish sauce
	15 ml (1 tbsp) sugar

Method

1

Heat the oil in a wok and fry the garlic and shallots, until beginning to soften. Add the chicken strips and stir-fry until they change colour.

2

Add the ginger, lime leaves, almonds, beans, pepper and water chestnuts.

3

Stir-fry, tossing the ingredients frequently, for 5 minutes, or until vegetables are cooked but still crisp. Stir in the fish sauce and sugar, and serve.

Serving suggestion

Serve with Thai Steamed Rice (page 66), boiled rice or cooked egg noodles.

Variation

Use unsalted roasted cashew nuts in place of the almonds.

Cook's tip

Cut the chicken across the grain to keep it tender during cooking.

Yellow Chicken Curry (Kaeng Karri Kai)

This easy-to-prepare curry illustrates the Indian influence on traditional Thai cuisine.

Preparation time: 10 minutes • Cooking time: 30-40 minutes • Serves: 4

Ingredients

450 g (1 lb) chicken breast, skinned and boned	45 ml (3 tbsp) Yellow Curry Paste (page 60)
30 ml (2 tbsp) oil	600 ml (1 pint) thick coconut milk (see 'Cook's tip', page 32)
2 cloves garlic, sliced	1 small potato, peeled and cut into chunks
1 onion, peeled and cut into wedges	2 kaffir lime leaves, shredded

Method

1

Cut the chicken into even-sized chunks.

2

Heat the oil in a wok and fry the garlic and onion for 3 minutes, then stir in the curry paste and fry for 1 minute.

3

Stir in half the coconut milk and bring to the boil. Boil rapidly for 5 minutes, stirring occasionally. Stir in the remaining coconut milk, bring to the boil and add the potatoes and chicken.

4

Reduce the heat and simmer gently for 20-30 minutes, or until the chicken is cooked and the potato is tender.

5

Spoon into serving dishes and sprinkle with the shredded lime leaves.

Serving suggestion

Serve with Stir-Fried Thai Noodles (page 74).

Variation

Use a sweet potato in place of the ordinary potato.

Barbecued Pork

Traditionally, this dish would be cooked on charcoal burners by the roadside, but it works just as well in the oven.

Preparation time: 15 minutes, plus 1 hour marinating time • Cooking time: 20 minutes • Serves: 4

Ingredients

4 cloves garlic, crushed	*2 pork fillets*
150 ml (¼ pint) light soy sauce	*30 ml (2 tbsp) oil*
55 g (2 oz) dark muscovado sugar	*2 shallots, chopped*
15 ml (1 tbsp) grated root ginger	*115 g (4 oz) ground roasted peanuts*
15 ml (1 tbsp) chopped fresh coriander stems and leaves	*150 ml (¼ pint) pork or chicken stock*
4 whole star anise or 5 ml (1 tsp) ground anise	*5 ml (1 tsp) cornflour, mixed with a little water*
Red food colouring (optional)	*Lime leaves and star anise, to garnish*

Method

1

Mix together the garlic, soy sauce, sugar, ginger, coriander, anise and a few drops of food colouring, if wished, to make a marinade.

2

Place the pork fillets in a shallow dish and add the marinade. Turn the pork over so that it is fully coated and leave to marinate for at least 1 hour, turning once.

3

Remove the meat from the marinade and place on a trivet in a roasting tin. Roast in an oven preheated to 375°F/190°C/Gas Mark 5 for 20 minutes, or until the pork is cooked. Baste once or twice with some of the marinade during cooking. Test the pork with a skewer – the juices should run clear.

4

Just before the end of the roasting time, heat the oil in a wok and fry the shallots until tender and beginning to brown. Stir in the ground peanuts, the remaining marinade and the stock. Cook until simmering, then stir in the cornflour mixture and cook a little longer until thickened.

5

To serve, slice the pork and pour the sauce over. Garnish with lime leaves and star anise.

Serving suggestion
Serve with Thai Fried Rice (page 68).

Variation
The pork can be cooked on a barbecue.

Chicken with Chilli and Basil

Three kinds of basil are used in Thailand, but Bai Horapa is the nearest to European basil. Look out for the other Thai varieties in Asian shops.

Preparation time: 20 minutes • Cooking time: 20 minutes • Serves: 4

Ingredients

4 chicken quarters	*2 green chillies, sliced*
3 large red chillies, seeded and chopped	*30 ml (2 tbsp) fish sauce*
15 ml (1 tbsp) fresh coriander stems and leaves	*15 ml (1 tbsp) oyster sauce (optional)*
2 cloves garlic, crushed	*A small bunch basil, torn into small pieces*
45 ml (3 tbsp) oil	*Chilli flowers (see 'Cook's tip', page 14), to garnish*

Method

1
Cut the chicken into smaller pieces using a large sharp knife or a meat cleaver.

2
Using a pestle and mortar, pound the red chillies, coriander and garlic together.

3
Heat the oil in a wok and fry the chicken until golden and almost cooked through. Remove from the pan.

4
Add the pounded chilli mixture and fry for a few minutes. Return the chicken to the pan and add the green chillies, fish sauce and oyster sauce, if using. Cook over a medium heat for 5-10 minutes, or until the chicken is completely cooked.

5
Stir in the basil leaves and serve garnished with chilli flowers.

Serving suggestion
Serve with Mixed Vegetable Stir-Fry (page 86).

Cook's tip
Tearing basil leaves rather than cutting them with a knife allows more flavour to be released.

Green and Red Curry Pastes

Red and green curry pastes are the basis of most Thai curries. Red curry paste is milder than the green.

Preparation time: 15 minutes for each paste • Makes: 45-60 ml (3-4 tbsp)

Ingredients

For the Green Curry Paste	For the Red Curry Paste
16 green Serrano or other small chillies, chopped	12 small red chillies, chopped
3 cloves garlic, crushed	3 cloves garlic, crushed
2 stems lemon grass, roughly chopped	1 stem lemon grass, chopped
3 spring onions, chopped	1 small onion, finely chopped
5 ml (1 tsp) grated root ginger	5 ml (1 tsp) grated root ginger
5 ml (1 tsp) coriander seeds	10 ml (2 tsp) chopped coriander stems and leaves
5 ml (1 tsp) caraway seeds	A large pinch of cumin
4 whole cloves	5 ml (1 tsp) shrimp paste
5 ml (1 tsp) ground nutmeg	30 ml (2 tbsp) oil
5 ml (1 tsp) shrimp paste	
45 ml (3 tbsp) oil	

Method

1

To make either the red or green curry paste, using a pestle and mortar, pound the chillies, garlic, lemon grass and onion until the mixture is well bruised and the juices begin to blend.

2

Add all the remaining ingredients, except the oil, and continue to pound until a paste is formed. Finally blend in the oil.

3

The curry pastes can also be made in a mini food processor – the quantity is too small for a full-size blender or processor. Place all the ingredients in the processor and grind to a paste.

Cook's tip

The pastes will keep for up to 1 month in the refrigerator. Store in an airtight jar.

Yellow Curry Paste

The turmeric in this paste gives curries a lovely golden hue. It has less heat than either the red or the green curry pastes.

Preparation time: 15 minutes • Makes: 75-90 ml (5-6 tbsp)

Ingredients

30 ml (2 tbsp) cumin seeds	5 ml (1 tsp) salt
30 ml (2 tbsp) coriander seeds	3 cloves garlic, crushed
3 stems lemon grass, chopped	1 small shallot, finely chopped
15 ml (1 tbsp) grated root ginger	5 ml (1 tsp) ground turmeric
6 red chillies, seeded and chopped	5 ml (1 tsp) shrimp paste

Method

1

Place the cumin and coriander seeds in a wok without any oil and dry-fry for 3-4 minutes, shaking the wok frequently to prevent the spices from burning. Remove from the heat and set aside.

2

Using a pestle and mortar, pound the lemon grass and ginger together until well crushed. Add the chillies and salt, and continue pounding together for about 4 minutes.

3

Add the garlic and shallot, and pound until broken down, then add the fried spices and turmeric. Finally, add the shrimp paste and continue to pound together until a smooth moist paste is produced.

Cook's tip

Store the paste in an airtight jar in the refrigerator until required. The paste will keep for up to 1 month.

Nam Prik

This is a hot dipping sauce which can be served with most Thai dishes, but is particularly good served with relatively mild dishes.

Preparation time: 10 minutes • Makes: 75-90 ml (5-6 tbsp)

Ingredients

5 ml (1 tsp) shrimp paste	5 small red chillies, chopped
5 ml (1 tsp) salt	8 anchovy fillets, chopped
5 ml (1 tsp) light muscovado sugar	10 ml (2 tsp) light soy sauce
4 cloves garlic, crushed	Juice of ½ lime

Method

1

Using a pestle and mortar, pound together the shrimp paste, salt, sugar, garlic, chillies and anchovies to a smooth paste, or process in a mini food processor.

2

Stir in the soy sauce and lime juice, and transfer to a small serving dish.

Serving suggestion

Serve with Pork Wrapped in Noodles (page 16) or Mixed Vegetable Stir-Fry (page 86).

Sweet Chilli Sauce

A delicious tangy sweet-and-sour chilli sauce.

Preparation time: 10 minutes • Serves: 4

Ingredients

115 g (4 oz) canned plums (drained weight), seeded	*1 clove garlic, crushed*
	5 ml (1 tsp) palm sugar
15 ml (1 tbsp) oil	*30 ml (2 tbsp) white wine vinegar*
3 red chillies, chopped	*Fish sauce, to taste*

Method

1

Chop the plums very finely. This can be done in a food processor if you wish.

2

Heat the oil in a small pan or wok, and fry the chillies and garlic for 3 minutes, until just softened.
Stir in the remaining ingredients and heat through.

Serving suggestion

Serve with Thai Spring Rolls (page 12) and other similar snacks or starters.

Sweet-and-Sour Dipping Sauce

Another popular dipping sauce that is ideal served with many Thai dishes.

Preparation time: 10 minutes • Serves: 4

Ingredients

55 g (2 oz) cucumber	*55 g (2 oz) palm sugar*
25 g (1 oz) carrots, peeled	*5 ml (1 tsp) chopped fresh coriander*
150 ml (¼ pint) white wine vinegar	

Method

1

Cut the cucumber and carrots into very small dice.

2

Combine with all the other ingredients in a bowl and stir until the sugar dissolves.

Cook's tip

This sauce is best served freshly made.

Fish Sauce with Chilli

As well as being used as a dipping sauce, this can be used in curries and stir-fries
to add spiciness and saltiness to the dish.

Preparation time: 5 minutes, plus 30 minutes standing time • Serves: 4

Ingredients

60 ml (4 tbsp) fish sauce	*6 small green chillies,*
15 ml (1 tbsp) lime juice	*sliced into circles*
2.5 ml (½ tsp) palm sugar	*½ small shallot, finely chopped*

Method

1

Combine the fish sauce and lime juice together in a small bowl. Add the sugar and stir until dissolved.

2

Add the prepared chillies and shallot, and stir until well combined. Leave to stand for at least 30 minutes before using.

Serving suggestion

Serve as a dipping sauce or over rice.

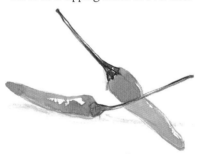

Nuoc Cham

This sauce is delicious served with rice or Spicy Prawn Wraps (page 18).

Preparation time: 10 minutes • Serves: 4

Ingredients

15 ml (1 tbsp) lime juice	*1 red chilli, seeded and shredded*
60 ml (4 tbsp) fish sauce	*15 ml (1 tbsp) grated carrot*
45 ml (3 tbsp) water	*15 ml (1 tbsp) chopped roasted*
5 ml (1 tsp) palm sugar	*peanuts*

Method

1

Combine the lime juice, fish sauce and water in a small bowl and add the sugar. Stir until the sugar dissolves.

2

Add the chilli and grated carrot, then stir in the roasted peanuts.

Cook's tip

This sauce is best served freshly made.

Thai Steamed Rice

Thai jasmine rice is a fragrant rice with a delicate flavour. Do not add salt during cooking, sine this will destroy the slightly nutty flavour.

Preparation time: 5 minutes • Cooking time: 40 minutes • Serves: 4-6

Ingredients

225 g (8 oz) jasmine rice	*600 ml (1 pint) water*

Method

1
Rinse the rice under running water and drain.

2
Place the rice and the measured water in a saucepan, and bring to the boil.

3
Stir in the rice and cover. Reduce the heat and simmer gently for 10 minutes, or until the water has been absorbed.

4
Line a bamboo steamer with a piece of muslin and pile the rice into the steamer. Cover and place the bamboo steamer over a large saucepan or wok of gently simmering water and steam for 30 minutes.

5
Leave the rice to stand for a few minutes, then fluff up gently with a fork.

Serving suggestion
Serve as an accompaniment to a Thai curry.

Thai Fried Rice (Khao Pad)

A flavourful rice dish combining prawns, chicken and vegetables.

Preparation time: 15 minutes • Cooking time: 15 minutes • Serves: 4-6

Ingredients

A little oil	15 ml (1 tbsp) Red or Green Curry Paste (page 58)
1 egg, beaten	30 ml (2 tbsp) fish sauce
15 ml (1 tbsp) thin coconut milk (see 'Cook's tip', page 32)	675 g (1½ lb) cooked rice
115 g (4 oz) chicken breasts, skinned and cut into small pieces	115 g (4 oz) long beans, cut into 2.5-cm (1-inch) lengths
115 g (4 oz) raw shelled prawns	6 spring onions, sliced diagonally
1 small red or green chilli, seeded and chopped	Chilli flowers, to garnish (see 'Cook's tip', page 14)

Method

1

Heat a wok and brush with a little oil. Beat together the egg and coconut milk, and pour into the wok. Swirl so that the egg coats it, to form a thin omelette.

2

Cook for a minute, until just brown on the underside, then flip over and cook the other side.

3

Remove from the wok and allow to cool slightly. Roll up and cut into thin strips. Set aside.

4

Heat a little more oil in the wok and add the chicken and prawns. Cook quickly, stirring frequently.

5

Add the chilli, curry paste and fish sauce to the pan, and heat until sizzling hot. Stir in the rice, beans and spring onions.

6

Reduce the heat slightly and cook, stirring constantly, until the rice is hot.

7

Pile into a serving dish and garnish with the shredded omelette and chilli flowers. Serve immediately.

Variation

Use a variety of different fresh vegetables of your choice in this dish, or those you have to hand.

Cook's tip

Before using the cooked rice, cool it by spreading out on a clean tea-towel, which will also absorb all the excess moisture.

Thai Rice Salad (Khao Yam)

An elegant and delicious salad from southern Thailand.

Preparation time: 20 minutes • Serves: 4

Ingredients

350 g (12 oz) cooked rice	55 g (2 oz) dried shrimps, chopped
½ cucumber	2 stems lemon grass, thinly sliced
1 grapefruit	
6 spring onions	**For the sauce**
2.5-cm (1-inch) piece root ginger	125 ml (4 fl oz) fish sauce
55 g (2 oz) shredded coconut	60 ml (4 tbsp) lime juice
55 g (2 oz) bean sprouts	30 ml (2 tbsp) muscovado sugar

Method

1

Divide the rice into 4 and press a quarter of the rice into a ramekin dish or tea cup. Turn out onto an individual serving plate. Repeat with the remaining rice.

2

Cut the cucumber into quarters and slice thinly. Cut off all the peel and pith of the grapefruit and segment the flesh. Slice the spring onions diagonally. Peel the ginger and cut into thin sticks.

3

Arrange the different salad ingredients separately on a serving platter. Combine the ingredients for the sauce and pour into 1 large or 4 small dishes.

4

Each diner should scatter some of the individual ingredients over their mound of rice and then drizzle the sauce over the top.

Variation

The salad ingredients can be mixed together and tossed in the sauce just before serving.

Cook's tip

Dried shrimps are tiny shrimps that have been boiled and then sun-dried. They are best stored in airtight glass jars, since they have a very pungent smell. Used extensively in Thai cooking, they are widely available from Oriental food stores.

Spicy Rice with Chicken

This tasty rice dish can be served on its own as a light lunch or supper dish.

Preparation time: 10 minutes • Cooking time: 15 minutes • Serves: 4

Ingredients

225 g (8 oz) cooked chicken	*450 g (1 lb) cooked rice*
115 g (4 oz) long beans, cut into 2.5-cm (1-inch) lengths	*30 ml (2 tbsp) fish sauce*
	5 ml (1 tsp) palm sugar
15 ml (1 tbsp) oil	*Chilli flowers (see 'Cook's tip', page 14) and spring onions, to garnish*
30 ml (2 tbsp) Red Curry Paste (page 58)	

Method

1

Cut the chicken into thin shreds. Blanch the beans in boiling water for 5 minutes, or until just tender.

2

Heat the oil in a wok and fry the curry paste for 3-4 minutes, stirring frequently.

3

Add the chicken and rice to the wok, and stir-fry for 5 minutes, tossing frequently.

4

Add the beans and cook a further 2 minutes, or until all the ingredients are piping hot.

5

Mix together the fish sauce and sugar, and stir until the sugar dissolves. Add to the wok. Toss well and serve garnished with chilli flowers and spring onions. Serve immediately.

Variations

Use cooked pork in place of the chicken. Use oyster sauce in place of the fish sauce.

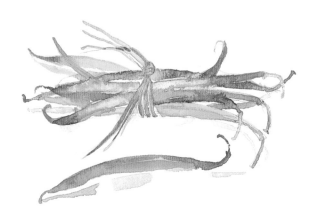

Stir-Fried Thai Noodles (Pad Thai)

This is a well-known basic Thai dish with as many variations as there are Thai cooks.

Preparation time: 10 minutes, plus 10-15 minutes soaking time • Cooking time: 15 minutes • Serves: 4

Ingredients

175 g (6 oz) rice noodles	15 ml (1 tbsp) soy sauce
60 ml (4 tbsp) oil	30 ml (2 tbsp) tamarind juice
225 g (8 oz) tofu, cut into cubes	2 eggs, beaten
3 cloves garlic, crushed	15 ml (1 tbsp) chopped garlic chives
55 g (2 oz) dried shrimps	55 g (2 oz) roasted peanuts, chopped
45 ml (3 tbsp) chopped pickled turnip	
60 ml (4 tbsp) fish sauce	225 g (2 oz) bean sprouts
25 g (1 oz) palm sugar	Chilli strips, to garnish

Method

1

Soak the rice noodles in boiling water for 10-15 minutes, or until softened. Drain and set aside.

2

Heat the oil in a wok and fry the tofu cubes until browned on all sides. Remove with a slotted spoon and set aside.

3

Add the garlic and dried shrimps to the wok, and stir-fry for 2 minutes. Reduce the heat and add the noodles.
Cook for 5 minutes, tossing the ingredients frequently. Add the pickled turnip, fish sauce, sugar, soy sauce
and tamarind juice, and cook for 2 minutes.

4

Add the beaten eggs and cook, tossing the ingredients together until the egg sets. Stir in the tofu, garlic chives, peanuts
and bean sprouts. Garnish with chilli strips and serve immediately.

Variations

Use unsalted cashew nuts in place of the peanuts. Use sliced bamboo shoots in place of the bean sprouts.

Cook's tip

Tamarind gives a fruity-sour flavour to dishes. Tamarind pulp is available in blocks from Oriental food stores.
To extract the juice, using about 1 part tamarind pulp to 2 parts water, soak the pulp in warm water for about 20-30 minutes.
Mash occasionally against the side of the boil. Strain through a sieve, pressing the juice out of the pulp with a spoon.
Scrape the underside of the sieve and add to the liquid. It is best used the same day.

Stir-Fried Glass Noodles with Chicken

Serve as part of a Thai meal, or as a light supper or snack for 2-3 people.

Preparation time: 5 minutes, plus 20 minutes marinating time • Cooking time: 15 minutes • Serves: 4

Ingredients

1 chicken breast, skinned and boned	*2.5 ml (½ tsp) grated root ginger*
30 ml (2 tbsp) oyster sauce	*175 g (6 oz) cellophane noodles*
30 ml (2 tbsp) fish sauce	*30 ml (2 tbsp) oil*
15 ml (1 tbsp) soy sauce	*2 cloves garlic, crushed*
5 ml (1 tsp) palm sugar	*1 red onion, sliced*
½ large red chilli, seeded and chopped	*Coriander leaves, to garnish*

Method

1

Cut the chicken into thin slices. In a shallow dish, combine the oyster, fish sauce, soy sauce, sugar, chilli and ginger. Add the chicken and toss until well coated. Leave to marinate for 20 minutes.

2

Soak the noodles in boiling water for 5 minutes, until softened. Drain and set aside.

3

Heat the oil in a wok and fry the garlic and onion until just softened. Add the chicken and the marinade, and stir-fry for about 10 minutes, or until the chicken is cooked through.

4

Add the noodles to the wok and toss over a low heat until heated through. Pile onto a serving dish and garnish with coriander leaves.

Variation

Use pork in place of the chicken.

Cook's tip

Partially freeze the chicken to make slicing easier. Cut the chicken across the grain to keep the meat tender during cooking.

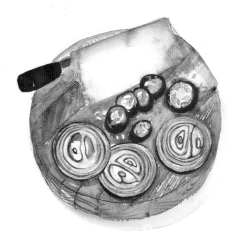

Tofu with Crispy Noodles

Tofu is ideal for making vegetarian main courses, since it can be used to replace meat or fish.

Preparation time: 10 minutes • Cooking time: 10 minutes • Serves: 4

Ingredients

Oil for deep-frying	*1 onion, peeled and cut into wedges*
115 g (4 oz) rice noodles (vermicelli)	*5 ml (1 tsp) shrimp paste*
225 g (8 oz) tofu, drained and patted dry	*30 ml (2 tbsp) light soy sauce*
2 carrots, peeled and sliced	*45 ml (3 tbsp) white wine vinegar*
85 g (3 oz) broccoli florets	*30 ml (2 tbsp) dark muscovado sugar*
2 sticks celery, sliced	*5 ml (1 tsp) root ginger*

Method

1

Heat the oil to 180°C/360°F in a wok. Add the rice noodles in small batches, turn over and fry for a few seconds. The noodles will puff up immediately.

2

Remove from the oil and drain well on absorbent kitchen paper.

3

Cut the tofu into cubes and fry for a few minutes until browned on all sides. Remove from the oil and set aside.

4

Pour off moist of the oil, add the carrots, broccoli, celery and onion to the wok and stir-fry for 2 minutes, or until the vegetables are cooked but still crisp.

5

Stir in the shrimp paste, soy sauce, vinegar, sugar and ginger. Return the vermicelli and tofu to the wok, toss to mix and serve immediately.

Variation

Use smoked tofu in place of the ordinary tofu, for a stronger flavoured dish.

Cook's tip

Rice noodles, as their name indicates, are made from rice, and are available dried in a variety of different sizes.

Long Beans in Coconut Milk

In this recipe, long beans are lightly cooked so that they are still slightly crunchy when served.

Preparation time: 10 minutes • Cooking time: 7 minutes • Serves: 4-6

Ingredients

450 g (1 lb) long beans	*1 large red chilli, seeded and chopped*
15 ml (1 tbsp) oil	*300 ml ($\frac{1}{2}$ pint) thin coconut milk* *(see 'Cook's tip', page 32)*
2 stems lemon grass, sliced	
2.5-cm (1-inch) piece galangal, sliced into thin sticks	*Chilli flowers (see 'Cook's tip, page 14), to garnish*

Method

1

Top and tail the beans and cut into 5-cm (2-inch) pieces.

2

Heat the oil in a wok and stir-fry the lemon grass, galangal and chilli for 1 minute.

3

Add the coconut milk and bring to the boil. Boil for 3 minutes.

4

Stir in the beans, reduce the heat and simmer for 6 minutes. Garnish with chilli flowers and serve immediately.

Serving suggestion

Serve as an accompaniment to a Thai main course dish.

Variation

Use mangetout in place of the long beans and reduce the cooking time to 2-3 minutes.

Sautéed Bean Sprouts

A simple vegetable dish with lots of texture. The prawns are an optional addition.

Preparation time: 5 minutes • Cooking time: 5 minutes • Serves: 4

Ingredients

30 ml (2 tbsp) oil	115 g (4 oz) cooked shelled prawns (optional)
8 spring onions, thickly sliced	½ small head Chinese cabbage, shredded
350 g (12 oz) canned bean sprouts, rinsed and drained	15 ml (1 tbsp) fish sauce

Method

1

Heat the oil in a wok until sizzling, then add the spring onions, bean sprouts and prawns, if using. Stir-fry for 1-2 minutes.

2

Add the Chinese cabbage and toss over a high heat for about 1 minute, or until just beginning to wilt.

3

Stir in the fish sauce and serve immediately.

Serving suggestion

Serve with a hot dipping sauce (see pages 60-64 for recipes) or as a foil to a hot curry.

Variation

Use fresh bean sprouts in place of the canned variety for a crunchier texture.

Cucumber Salad

Salads are an important part of a Thai meal. They are usually carefully arranged rather than simply tossed together.

Preparation time: 10 minutes • Serves: 4

Ingredients

1 cucumber	**For the dressing**
A few lettuce leaves, washed	*30 ml (2 tbsp) lime juice*
1 red pepper, sliced	*15 ml (1 tbsp) fish sauce*
25 g (1 oz) roasted peanuts	*5 ml (1 tsp) sugar*
	1 small red or green chilli, seeded and chopped
	10 ml (2 tsp) chopped coriander leaves

Method

1

Cut the cucumber in half lengthways and scoop out the seeds with a teaspoon.

2

Cut the cucumber into slices about 5 mm (¼ inch) thick.

3

Arrange the lettuce leaves on a serving plate, then scatter the sliced pepper around the edge.
Pile the cucumber into the centre. Sprinkle with the roasted peanuts.

4

To make the dressing, whisk all the ingredients together with a fork, or place in a small screw-top jar and shake well.

5

Just before serving, drizzle the dressing over the salad.

Variation

Use cashew nuts in place of the peanuts.

Cook's tip

Do not add the dressing to the salad until just before serving.

Mixed Vegetable Stir-Fry

The freshness and texture of vegetables is retained in stir-frying, to produce a colourful and flavoursome side dish.

Preparation time: 15 minutes • Cooking time: 4-6 minutes • Serves: 4

Ingredients

For the dipping sauce (Prik Dong)	
6 red or green chillies	1 small red pepper, sliced
90 ml (6 tbsp) white wine vinegar	115 g (4 oz) mangetout
30 ml (2 tbsp) oil	115 g (4 oz) baby corn
3 cloves garlic, crushed	115 g (4 oz) long beans, cut into 5-cm (2-inch) lengths
1 shallot, sliced	2 carrots, peeled and sliced
85 g (3 oz) each cauliflower and broccoli, divided into small florets	85 g (3 oz) straw mushrooms
	10 ml (2 tsp) palm sugar
	15 ml (1 tbsp) light soy sauce

Method

1

To make the dipping sauce, slice the chillies diagonally and combine with the vinegar in a small bowl.

2

Heat the oil in a wok and add all the vegetables at once.

3

Stir-fry for 4 minutes, until the vegetables are cooked but still crisp.

4

Stir the sugar into the soy sauce and add to the wok. Toss well and serve with the dipping sauce.

Serving suggestion

Serve the dipping sauce with noodles as well as with other vegetable dishes.

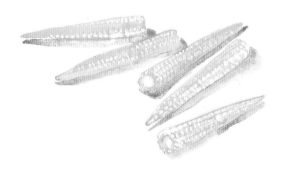

Thai Fruit Platter with Coconut Sauce

Customarily, a Thai meal will finish with fresh fruit. In this recipe, a selection of fruit is served with a simple coconut sauce.

Preparation time: 20-30 minutes • Serves: 4

Ingredients

A selection of Thai fruit, such as:	
Lychees	Star fruit
Rambutans	Bananas
Mango	A little lemon juice
Pineapple	**For the coconut sauce**
Watermelon	175 ml (6 fl oz) thick coconut milk
Honeydew melon	(see 'Cook's tip', page 32)
Papaya	55 g (2 oz) caster sugar

Method

1
Prepare the fruit. Peel lychees or rambutans, starting at the stem end.

2
Cut the mango in half either side of the stone. Peel and slice into fingers.

3
Cut the pineapple into wedges and peel.

4
Slice the star fruit crosswise.

5
Cut the bananas diagonally into chunks and toss in lemon juice.

7
Arrange the fruit on a serving platter.

8
To make the sauce, combine the coconut milk with the sugar. Pour over the fruit or serve separately in a bowl or jug.

Serving suggestion
If serving the sauce separately, garnish with grated lemon and lime zest. Chill the fruit and sauce before serving, if you wish.

Thai Coconut Custards

This is one of the best known and most loved Thai desserts.

Preparation time: 5 minutes • Cooking time: 30-40 minutes • Serves: 6

Ingredients

4 eggs	2.5 ml (½ tsp) jasmine water
425 ml (¾ pint) thick coconut milk (see 'Cook's tip', page 32)	Desiccated coconut, grated lime zest and lime twists, to decorate
115 g (4 oz) caster sugar	

Method

1

Place the eggs, coconut milk, sugar and jasmine water in a bowl and whisk together until slightly frothy.

2

Pour into a shallow heatproof dish that will fit into the top of a bamboo steamer.

3

Cover, place the steamer over a large saucepan or wok of gently simmering water and steam for 30-40 minutes, or until the custard is just set. If the custard cooks too quickly, it will become rubbery in texture.

4

Remove from the steamer and allow to cool. Cut into wedges or blocks, and decorate with the coconut, grated lime zest and lime twists.

Cook's tips

The custard is cooked when the tip of a knife blade inserted into the centre comes out clean. Jasmine water is used in Thai cooking in the same way as rosewater or orange flower water in Indian cuisine. It is made from the flowers of a highly scented type of jasmine, and adds a perfumed fragrance to dishes.

Coconut and Banana Pancakes

These pancakes are equally delicious served warm or cold.

Preparation time: 15 minutes, plus 20 minutes standing time • Cooking time: 15 minutes • Serves: 4

Ingredients

115 g (4 oz) rice flour	**For the filling**
A pinch of salt	30 ml (2 tbsp) lime juice
2 eggs	Grated rind of ½ lime
300 ml (½ pint) thin coconut milk (see 'Cook's tip', page 32)	5 ml (1 tsp) sugar
Green food colouring (optional)	15 ml (1 tbsp) shredded or desiccated coconut
25 g (1 oz) shredded or desiccated coconut	
Oil, for frying	2 bananas

Method

1

Place the flour and the salt in a mixing bowl and make a well in the centre. Drop in the eggs and a little of the coconut milk.

2

Using a wooden spoon, beat well, slowly incorporating the flour until you have a smooth, thick paste.

3

Gradually beat in the remaining coconut milk. Stir in a few drops of food colouring if using. Allow to stand for 20 minutes.

4

Meanwhile, make the filling. Mix together the lime juice, rind, sugar and coconut. Slice the bananas and toss in the mixture.

5

Stir the coconut into the pancake batter and heat a little oil in a 20-cm (8-inch) heavy-based frying pan. Pour off the excess and spoon in about 60 ml (4 tbsp) of the batter. Swirl to coat the pan. Cook for about 1 minute, or until the underside is golden.

6

Flip or toss the pancake over and cook the other side. Slide the pancake out of the pan and keep warm. Repeat until all the batter is used. Fill the pancakes with the banana mixture and serve immediately.

Serving suggestion

Fold the pancakes into quarters and spoon some filling inside. Alternatively, divide the filling between the pancakes and roll up.

Mango Ice Cream

The cool, smooth creaminess of this delicious ice cream makes it the perfect end to a Thai meal.

Preparation time: 30 minutes, plus several hours freezing time • Cooking time: 10 minutes • Serves: 8

Ingredients

425 ml (³/4 pint) thick coconut milk (see 'Cook's tip', page 32)	*300 ml (¹/2 pint) double cream*
3 egg yolks	*3 mangoes, peeled and stoned*
60 ml (4 tbsp) sugar	*Toasted flaked almonds, to decorate*

Method

1
Heat the coconut milk in a saucepan until very hot but not boiling.

2
Beat together the egg yolks and sugar in a bowl, add a few spoons of the hot coconut milk and stir well.

3
Stir into the remaining coconut milk and cook gently over a saucepan of simmering water, stirring constantly
until it thickens enough to coat the back of a spoon.

4
Remove from the heat and cool. Whip the double cream until soft peaks form, then stir in the cooled custard.

5
Chop a little of the mango into small pieces and purée the remainder in a food processor or press through a sieve.

6
Fold the mango purée and chopped mango into the custard. Pour into a shallow, freezerproof dish and freeze until slushy.

7
Remove from the freezer and process in the food processor or beat with an electric whisk until smooth.
Freeze and beat once more, then transfer to a freezer container and cover with a lid. Freeze until solid.

8
Remove the ice cream about 20-30 minutes before serving and allow to soften in the refrigerator.
Scoop into dishes and serve sprinkled with toasted flaked almonds.

Serving suggestion
Serve with extra slices of mango, if you wish.

Cook's tips
Do not allow the coconut milk to boil, since the eggs will curdle when added. Beating the ice cream as it freezes breaks
up the ice crystals and makes the texture of the ice cream more smooth.

Index